MINDFULNESS JOURNAL

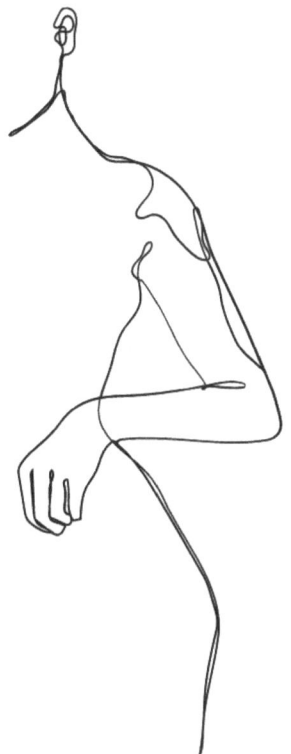

Walk in love

Copyright © 2021 by Rosalie Bardo

All rights reserved. This book or parts thereof may not be reproduced in any form, stored in any retrieval system, or transmitted in any form by any means—electronic, mechanical, photocopy, recording, or otherwise—without prior written permission of the publisher, except as provided by the United States of America copyright law. For permission requests, contact the publisher, at "Attention: Permissions Coordinator," at the address below.

GREYHOUSE PRESS

The intent of the author is to provide helpful information on the subjects discussed. Although the author has made every effort to ensure that the information in this book is true and correct to the best of our knowledge, the author does not assume and hereby disclaims any liability to any party for any loss, damage, or disruption caused by errors or omissions, whether such errors or omissions result from negligence, accident, or any other cause.

Library of Congress-in Publication-Data
Bardo, Rosalie
Ascend: Mindfulness Journal/ by Rosalie Bardo;
Interior Design by Rosalie Bardo
Summary: Mindfulness Journal with
meditative art, affirmations
and writing prompts
to assist in reframing your day.
124 pgs.
ISBN: 978-0-9978738-7-0

Printed in the United States of America
Distributed by: GreyHouse Press
Cover and book design by Rosalie Bardo
Cover font: Belleza/AmsterdamThree
Interior font: Belleza/AmsterdamThree

EVERY ACT CAN BE A
SPIRITUAL PRACTICE

MAKE
THE MUNDANE
SACRED

DO YOU VIEW LIFE LIKE A BATTLE OR CONSTANT STRUGGLE?

+ Lifting your veil + Do you have positive intentions +
Are your daily actions coming from a pure place?

_____
_____
_____
_____
_____
_____
_____
_____
_____
_____
_____
_____
_____

SHARE YOUR TRUTH WITH ME
_____
_____

WE ARE ALL CONNECTED.

ARE YOU OPEN AND RECEPTIVE TO ABSORBING KNOWLEDGE FROM THOSE AROUND YOU?

OBSERVE: GAIN FROM ANOTHER'S EXPERIENCE. WE ALL HAVE SOMETHING UNIQUE TO SHARE. ENGAGE THE WORLD WITH COMPASSION, PATIENCE AND GENEROSITY.

TELL ME ABOUT YOUR JOYFUL MOMENTS FROM THIS PAST YEAR

an encounter + discovering a new hobby + new connection

YOU ARE MAGICAL

LIST THE DAILY HABITS YOU KNOW YOU NEED TO WORK ON?

+ share your flaws +
+ acknowledge them +
+ continue holding space for radical self acceptance +

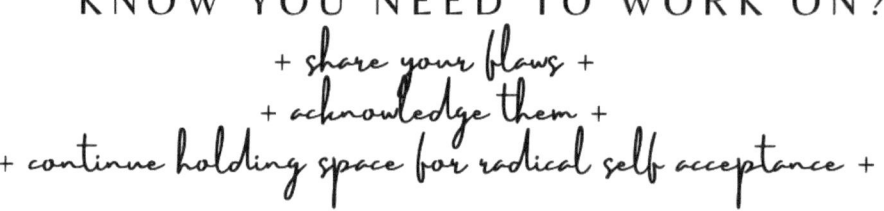

HOW OFTEN DO YOU PRETEND TO LIKE OR BE INTERESTED IN THINGS THAT ARE TRENDY IN HOPES OF FEELING LIKE YOU FIT IN?

Does it make you feel like a fraud?

LIST SOME UNIQUE INTERESTS WITHOUT THE CONCERN OF JUDGEMENT

WHAT DOES YOUR INNER VOICE SOUND LIKE?

Your tone? Condescending + Supportive + Calm
Are you kind to yourself?

_____
_____
_____
_____
_____
_____
_____
_____
_____
_____
_____
_____
_____
_____
_____

FORGIVE

ARE YOU HAPPY FOR OTHERS WHEN THEY ARE SUCCESSFUL OR DOES IT MAKE YOU FEEL INADEQUATE?

Write down your accomplishments and reflect on your own success.

CHILL FOR A MOMENT

CLOSE YOUR EYES

TAKE A FEW DEEP BREATHS

RELAX YOUR SHOULDERS

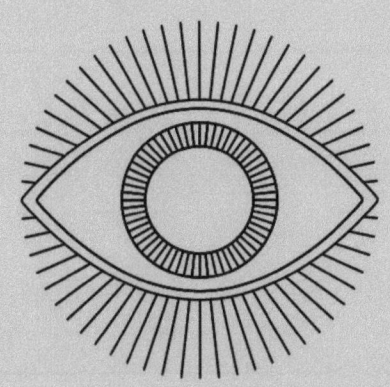

WHAT CAN YOU RELEASE?
+ LET GO +

WHAT MAKES YOU LAUGH?
belly laugh + giggle + chuckle

_____
_____
_____
_____
_____
_____
_____
_____
_____
_____
_____
_____

WHO MAKES YOU LAUGH?
_____
_____
_____
_____

ARE YOU GENUINELY LISTENING
WHEN PEOPLE SPEAK TO YOU?

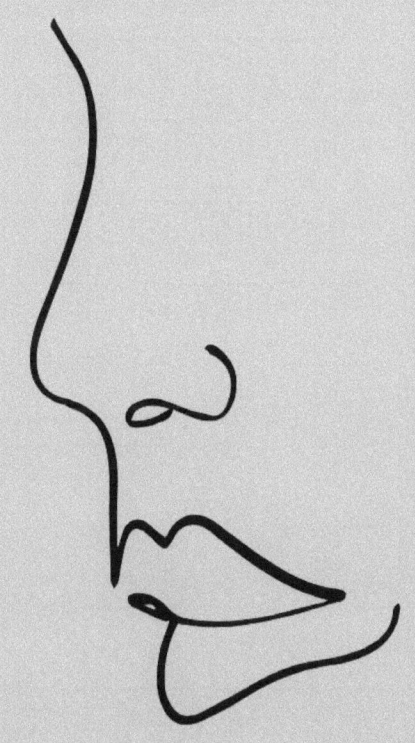

DO YOU FIND YOURSELF
DISTRACTED BY EGO
OR ARE YOU BEING
A SINCERE WITNESS,
PRESENT IN THE MOMENT?

REFLECT ON THE HELPERS IN YOUR LIFE

Who shows up for you + who is always there?

healing

+ the process of clarity +
becoming grounded, secure, the beautiful knowing.

DO YOU SPEND TIME REFLECTING ON THINGS YOU WISH YOU COULD CHANGE ABOUT THE PAST? *What would you change? Write it down, then let it go.*

YOU ARE

+

PHE·NOM·E·NAL

+ VERY REMARKABLE; ASTONISHING +

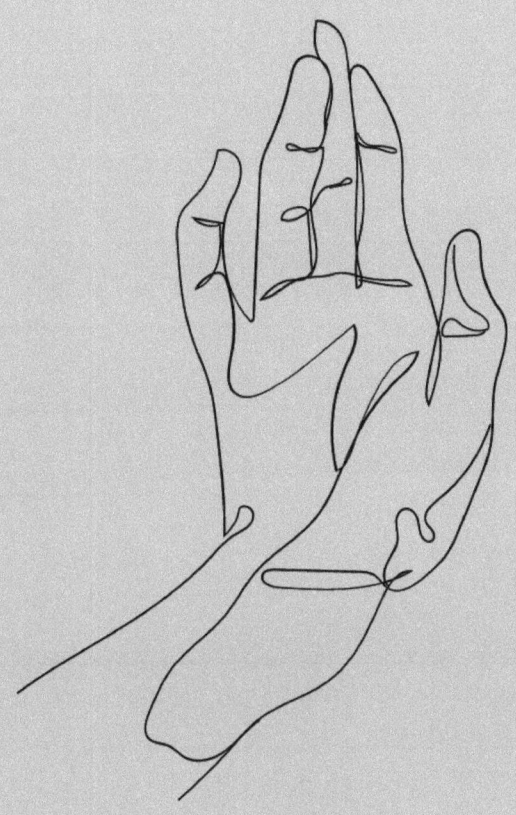

WHAT ARE YOU PASSIONATE ABOUT?

your job + your family + your pets + activism?
+ share the things that get you excited +

_____

_____

_____

_____

_____

_____

_____

_____

_____

_____

_____

_____

_____

ARE YOU LOOKING FORWARD
TO TOMORROW?

_____

_____

WHERE DO YOU SEE YOURSELF IN 3 YEARS?

WHAT ACTIONS ARE LIMITING YOU IN LIFE?

Negative thought patterns + Not getting enough sleep + Consuming unhealthy food + Hanging around unmotivated people

___
___
___
___
___
___
___
___
___
___
___
___
___
___
___
___
___
___

REMEMBER WHO YOU ARE

Go your own way

SPEAK ALOUD

I CAN DO HARD THINGS

I LOVE WHO I AM BECOMING

I RESPOND CALMLY

I ADAPT POSITIVELY TO CHANGE

I AM TOLERANT OF OTHERS

IN WHAT WAYS DO YOU REST?

+ meditate + read a book + binge watch TV + sleep during the day + scroll on your phone

---

ARE YOU TRULY IN A STATE OF REST? WHAT COULD YOU DO DIFFERENTLY TO ALLOW YOUR MIND & BODY TO REST?

WHAT SCARES YOU?

ARE YOUR FEARS RATIONAL OR DO YOU HAVE A TENDENCY TO OVERTHINK THINGS?

MET·A·MOR·PHO·SIS

A CHANGE OF THE NATURE OF A
BEING INTO A COMPLETELY
DIFFERENT ONE: BECOMING

DO YOU BELIEVE IN THE POWER OF SPEAKING DAILY AFFIRMATIONS?

begin a list, I'll start...

1. I AM HEALTHY

KEEP GOING.
READ YOUR LIST ALOUD

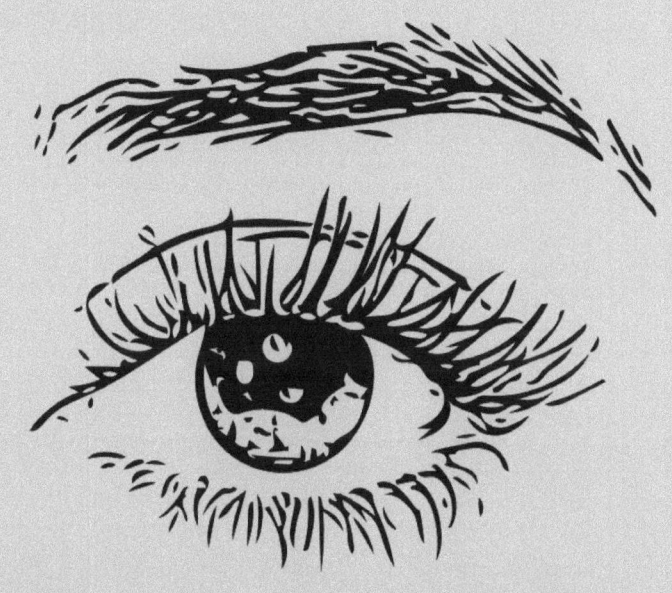

ARE YOU INSPIRED TO
EVOLVE OR DO YOU
FEEL CONTENT
WITH YOUR CURRENT
STATE OF BEING?

HOW DO YOU FEEL TODAY?
are you experiencing joy + depression + anxiety?
+ share your day with me +

___
___
___
___
___
___
___
___
___
___
___
___
___
___

WOULD YOU CHANGE ANYTHING ABOUT YOUR ROUTINE?

___
___

LOOK AROUND

DESCRIBE ONLY THE PLEASING THINGS YOU SEE.

WHAT ARE HEALTHY BOUNDARIES?
Do you remove people from your life when they continue to disrespect your boundaries?

NEVER SETTLE.
YOU ARE WORTHY OF RESPECT.

RESPECT YOURSELF

HOW OFTEN DO YOU CRY?

I AM CAPABLE

I AM CAPABLE

I AM CAPABLE

I AM CAPABLE

CA·PA·BLE

HAVING THE ABILITY OR STAMINA NECESSARY TO ACHIEVE A SPECIFIC THING.

SIMILAR:

HAVE WHAT IT TAKES TO

ABLE TO FOLLOW THROUGH EFFICIENTLY; SKILLFUL.

+ Make a list of your goals and aspirations +

_____

_____

_____

_____

_____

_____

_____

_____

_____

_____

_____

_____

_____

_____

_____

_____

CREATIVITY EXPLORE RESIST
WARRIOR SIMPLIFY
ENERGY ATTRACT ABUNDANCE
CALMNESS
WORDS HOLD POWER
GODDESS AWARE
fearless EXPANSION DIVINE
MOVEMENT PEACE WALK IN LOVE
SPEAK INTO EXISTENCE SACRED i am
receiving
eternal CONNECTION
EGO
EMPOWERED
TRUTH SELCOUTH PURE RESONATE
MEDITATION bliss
CLARITY
PROTECTION EMPATHY
INVITE THANK YOU
READY
BECOMING YES TRANSFORMATION
HEALING MANIFEST VAST QUESTION
ILLUMINATE
illusion TRUST purify
WRITE elated
ADAPT SUSTAINABLE

YOU. ARE. LOVED.

DO YOU EVER FEEL
ALONE OR LONELY?

WHY + WHY NOT?

*do you enjoy being alone or
do you crave the energy of others?*

YOU ARE WORTHY.
YOU HAVE NOTHING TO
PROVE.

SPEAK ALOUD

I am kind

I do not seek acceptance from others

I am emotionally healthy

I am a good friend

I am worthy of all good things

I focus on one task and complete it

I am grateful for this journey

I am abundant in every aspect of my life

REFLECT ON A TIME WHEN YOU WERE COURAGEOUS

WHAT DID THAT MOMENT FEEL LIKE? WHAT HAPPENED?

TELL ME ABOUT YOUR FRIENDS?

reflect on the common thread that connects you

WE ALL HAVE DREAMS, EVEN IF WE NEVER SHARE THEM.

WHAT ARE SOME DREAMS YOU'VE KEPT HIDDEN, BUT WOULD LOVE TO PURSUE?

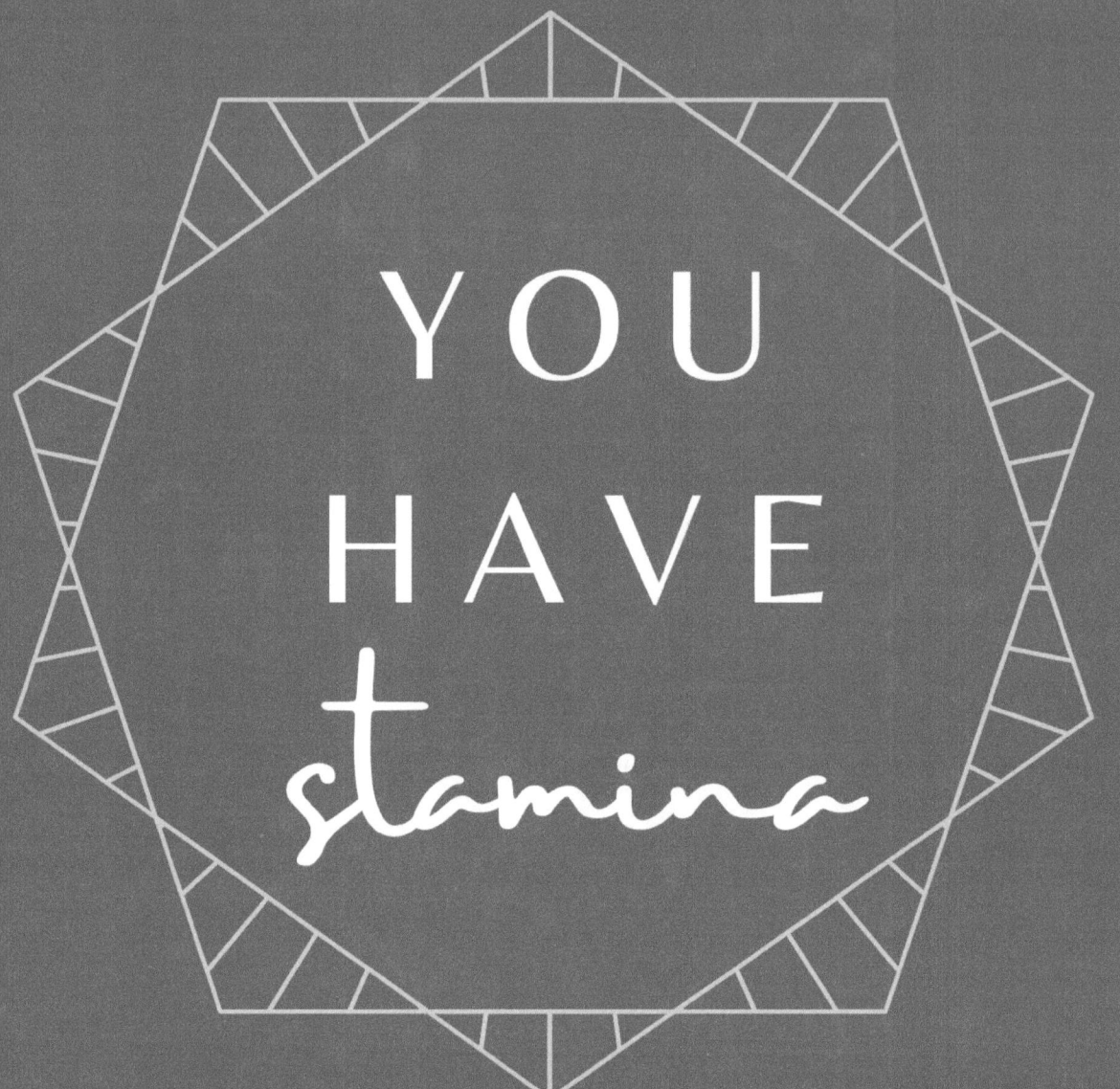

EXUDE

GRATITUDE

SHARE YOUR GRATITUDE

good health + creative outlets + relationships + experiences + job + Make a list

_____
_____
_____
_____
_____
_____
_____
_____
_____
_____
_____
_____
_____
_____
_____
_____

YOUR KINDNESS IS CONTAGIOUS

OBSERVE BUT DO NOT ABSORB.
PROTECT YOUR ENERGY

SPEAK ALOUD

I desire peace

I am free to do as I wish

I am successful in my endeavors

I am a good neighbor

I am worthy of all good things

I believe in myself and my abilities

I let go of past regrets

I am capable of CHANGE

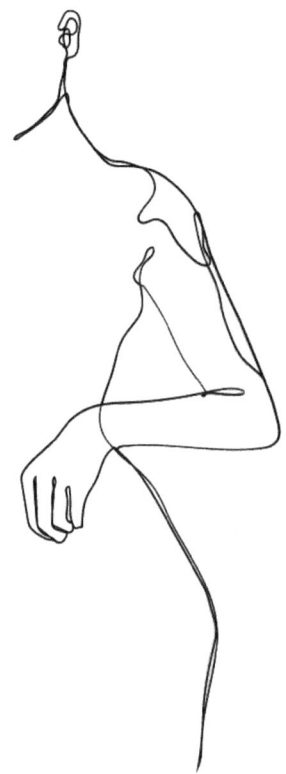

Continue walking, in love, with love

YOU ARE

+

SAFE

YOU ARE PROTECTED

www.ingramcontent.com/pod-product-compliance
Lightning Source LLC
Chambersburg PA
CBHW041432010526
44118CB00002B/52